Helena Olsen

PUBLISHED BY: Helena Olsen

Copyright © 2016 All rights reserved.

No part of this publication may be copied, reproduced in any format, by any means, electronic or otherwise, without prior consent from the copyright owner and publisher of this book.

Contents

Introduction

Hygge (pronounced "hoo-gah") is a mysterious-looking Danish word that has many meanings. Warmth, happiness, security, friendship, companionship, contentedness, coziness are just a few of the English words we could use to translate hygge. Hygge is the removal of things that cause stress in our lives – it is the ongoing pursuit of a simpler, healthier, more fulfilled and happier existence.

In my previous book, "How to Hygge", I wrote about hygge and its benefits, why it is such a powerful concept and the various aspects in your life into which you can bring hygge. This book explains how to create simple and effective five-minute habits that you can use, starting today, to fill your life with hygge. These habits are easy both to implement and follow and are all able to be completed within five minutes. They will allow you to avoid stressful and anxious moments and enjoy many more times of happiness and contentment with friends and family.

Each of these small, highly effective habits, can be performed as part of everyday life, whenever the opportunity arises. You don't need to implement all these habits at once. You can make these small changes one at time, creating simple to follow habits within your daily schedule or weekly plan.

The book contains 42 practical examples of how hygge can become part of your life. These examples range from ideas for you to carry out on an individual level, to creating stronger relationships with friends and family to adapting your living spaces, to getting the most out of both work and play and more.

I have talked about hygge for many years on both a personal and professional level and have continued to enjoy the benefits it brings at all the various stages of my life. Hygge is part of who

I am, and it is something I try to add into every possible aspect of my life. It is my aim to give you a resource of easy hygge habits that you can use, to do exactly the same.

This resource of habits will enable you to feel less-stressed, happier and more content, filling your day with all the positive effects that a hygge lifestyle can bring. All these simple hygge habits are explained in detail in the following pages.

After reading this book, you will be able to implement quick and easy, practical changes, starting today, that will create highly beneficial hygge habits in your own life. By making these habits part of your routine and be embedding the very notion of hygge into all that you do, you allow hygge and all its associated benefits to be part of your life and that of your friends and families. Let's get started.

Hygge and your Surroundings (Habits #1 to #9)

Most of us spend a considerable amount of time in our homes. Your home should always provide a source of joy and inspiration as well as offering you warmth and shelter. Your home should be a place of happiness and comfort. Your living space should be able to give you every opportunity to add more hygge to your life.

This chapter contains several five-minute habits that you can start today to ensure your home will always be somewhere special to you. These habits will enable you to create a place where you can truly relax, enjoy your time with friends and family and create long-lasting joyful memories.

Habit #1 - Decluttering

Decluttering your home is the process of removing objects that you no longer enjoy or need and ensuring that every remaining item has its own place. A home that is freed from clutter will be less stressful for you as you won't be constantly worried whether everything is in its rightful place or not. Decluttering means you won't see hundreds of items in your home that serve only to divert your energy away from what is important.

You will feel more inclined to invite people to your home, to be more social, if you are not concerned that the house is messy and unwelcoming. You will have more time for family activities and hygge in general, if you are not always packing away things you no longer need or care for. You will be able to spend far less time tidying and cleaning the house and more time doing the things you enjoy.

The less you have, the less you need to worry about cleaning or dusting or moving around every single day. You can create more space and a more comfortable living environment, one that is more open to creating a hygge lifestyle, by eliminating those items that no longer warrant a place in your life.

There are many reasons why decluttering is such an important part of hygge. However, many people fail to start the process because the idea of going through all your possessions is utterly overwhelming. This is a reason why it's a great idea to get into the habit of decluttering just five minutes at a time. You will be amazed at how much you will be able to achieve over a week, a month or longer.

With your five minutes, concentrate on one particular area. If you are in the kitchen, look at a counter. If it holds old kitchen gadgets that you no longer use, clear them off and put them in a cupboard. If you haven't used them for many months, then they might be worth a few dollars to sell or you can just give them away.

If you're in a living room, then look at the coffee table or a shelf. Perhaps it has old newspapers or magazines or letters or dirty cups on it. Clear it all off so you have a fresh, clean surface to admire. Take a minute or two to allocate places for items you know you use often, but seem to move around all the time to wherever there happens to be a free space. Find the right space for them. Resolve to put these items back in that place every time you stop using them.

If it's papers or bills that are causing the mess, then take five minutes to label some folders and file them – one folder for bills for example. If the papers are old and won't be needed again, throw them away. You could scan the bills into your computer or take a photograph and then throw the papers away. Now you will have an electronic record which takes up no physical space at all.

Take five minutes to look at items in your wardrobe. If you've not worn items of clothing for months on end, then dispose of them. It won't take long before your wardrobe is purged of items that were of no use and were slowing you down when deciding what to wear.

In five minutes you could go through a drawer that always ends up with a load of junk in it. Somehow, all those little knick-knacks or old keys or mysterious items of hardware find their way into a drawer and reside there for years. In five minutes, you can throw anything away you know you will no longer use or need again.

There are many different ways you can start to declutter and great benefits in doing so. If you can get into the habit of carrying out a five minute declutter every day, you will very quickly find yourself reaping the rewards of a less cluttered and more welcoming and hyggeligt environment for the entire family.

Habit #2 - Lighting candles

There can be little more that is true hygge than lighting candles. The Danes love candles for the beautiful light they cast around the room and the intimacy they can create. Any space lit by candles takes on a much warmer and more inviting atmosphere. Candles can take all forms of shapes and sizes, but it is best to opt for natural candles made from beeswax to avoid the soot and chemicals that paraffin candles can release into the air.

Even if it takes just a couple of minutes to light four or five small tea-candles, you will find the room changes dramatically as other forms lighting can then be dimmed or even turned off entirely. If you are looking for a fast and easy way to provide hygge, then spending a little time lighting lovely candles is one of the best available options. This is an easy daily habit to get into. It takes even less than five minutes and creates a wonderfully warming and relaxing atmosphere in any room.

Habit #3 - Using effective lighting to relax

The right lighting is critical in establishing hygge in your home. Get into the habit of switching to a cozier and more inviting lighting set-up as evening creeps in and you look to relax after the day is over. If you want to go high-tech, there are even light bulbs and entire lighting systems that you can connect to your home network that will dim or cast a different color at different times of the day.

The overhead lights which you used during the day may illuminate the room brightly, however the light may be white and harsh which makes relaxing in the room difficult. Take a minute or two to ensure lamps replace overhead lights with their softer and more soothing light. Check they are placed at points of interest in the room, perhaps on a table where you can read in peace. If you have dimmer switches you can also use these to set the exact lighting level that you find the most relaxing.

Making it a habit to ensure living spaces are lit properly for the evening will create a more inviting atmosphere, where people will be keen to gather and share their stories of the day. This allows families and friends to spend time together and communicate effectively. It lets you relax more fully and rest your eyes, as well as creating a contrast between the harsher lights of the working day and the more intimate lighting of the evening.

Habit #4 - Bringing Nature inside

An essential part of hygge is ensuring there is more of the natural world into your life. You achieve this by bringing some of nature you find outside into your home. These elements of nature contain a vitality that can also make a room cozier and more inviting. These can be almost anything which you think would enhance the feel of your living spaces.

It might be flowers in a vase or perhaps a particularly interesting piece of bark or some twigs that might find place in your home. You could gather different sized and colored rocks or pebbles to make a beautiful collection in a bowl on a table. Perhaps a feather which you discover can be brought in. A collection of beautiful colored leaves can look stunning as a decoration. Not only do these items of natural beauty look wonderful, they also add different textures to the room.

Take five minutes each week to forage in your garden or the street outside your home or a local park to see what features of the natural world can be brought inside. It will add an instant touch of hygge and prove to be a free and stunning decoration to any room.

Habit #5 - Watering your plants

The importance of plants, at home or at work, for creating a hyggeligt atmosphere is difficult to overstate. Plants look beautiful and add to the ambience wherever they are placed, but they have an even more important role. They purify the air and remove toxins and pollutants. NASA conducted a study where it concluded that house plants were invaluable for their purification service. The report cites the Peace Lily, Chrysanthemum, Red-Edged Dracaena, Chinese Evergreen, and English Ivy as some of the plants to consider for your home.

Dedicate a couple of minutes in your day to look after your plants. This will take your thoughts away from other concerns or worries and make you focus on nurturing a living thing. This process relieves stress and boosts your mental performance. Caring for plants can also increase your feelings of empathy, making it easier to forge strong relationships with the people around you – a key facet of hygge.

Having plants around, looking after them and seeing them flourish has numerous beneficial effects, both physical and mental. Just five minutes a day spent looking after your plants will greatly increase your feeling of hygge as well as creating a beautiful home.

Habit #6 - Opening Windows

Coziness and warmth are essential for hygge, but that doesn't mean your home should be hermetically sealed with not a hint of fresh air allowed to enter. Allowing fresh air to enter your home will help prevent build-up of possible condensation and allow dust, mold spores and bacteria to escape. A home without fresh air coming in regularly will feel stuffy and stale.

Getting into the daily habit of opening your windows, even just for five minutes a day, can make a big difference to improving your indoor air quality. It is refreshing and revitalising, even in the colder weather, and you will feel much better for the cleaner and fresher air circulating around your home.

Habit #7 - Watching wildlife

One way to enjoy the benefits of nature and wildlife is to have a bird feeder which you can watch from inside your home. Simply place one in view of a window and add in seeds, peanuts, millet or suet cakes that you can pick up from the shops. There are various types of feeders ranging from the hopper feeder which is simply a platform with walls and a roof that covers the seed, to tube feeders or ones that use a type of cage into which you can place the suet cakes.

By attracting beautiful wildlife to your garden, you can have the benefit of enjoying the company of birds as well as helping to replace other food sources that have become more scarce over the years. In addition, there is the chance to interact with nature and learn more about the natural world. Five minutes spent looking at wildlife is a highly effective and enjoyable way to teach children about nature and can be a great experience for the entire family.

Habit #8 - Choosing photographs as decoration

If you are looking to decorate your walls, then one of the most effective ways you can achieve this is through photographs. Photographs bring back memories of fun times with friends or family and can hold a strong emotional significance for you. I have photographs of various sizes and in different styles of frame scattered throughout my house.

If you take digital photographs, you can add them to a digital photo frame which rotates the pictures at regular intervals. I prefer, however, to make a physical version of photos that I love, often blown up to a much larger size and printed on canvas, which I can then position on the wall wherever I choose. Adding lots of small photographs together to one portion of the wall or a shelf is also a highly effective way of decorating and can become an interesting talking point for guests.

You can create a rectangle from your collection of frames and try and combine both horizontal and vertical pictures within it. You can use different sizes and style of frames as well, within the same area. I have a friend who has an entire wall dedicated to photographs of her family on various holidays over the years making a highly attractive and interesting showpiece.

There are many different ways in which you can show photographs. It is a quick and highly effective way of decorating your living space. Not only is it a form of beautiful art which will have a positive effect upon you whenever you see it, but the photographs tell a fascinating story about who you are and who came before you. This gives a connection throughout generations which reinforces a sense of belonging for the entire family.

Spending a few minutes a week choosing new photographs to add in is a great activity either alone or with others. It gives a chance to remember and talk about the places or gatherings around which the photographs were taken and perhaps provides an opportunity to plan even more. It's a great hygge habit to get into each week and one everyone can enjoy.

Habit #9 - Tidying

It is difficult, if not impossible, to create a hyggeligt atmosphere when the environment around you is a mess. If you feel everything is out of its place, then you will be stressed and unable to fully relax at home or make progress at work. It can be difficult sometimes to fight the feeling of being overwhelmed when you look around an entire house. Nonetheless, you can do a great deal in a five-minute burst.

In five minutes, it is easy to concentrate on just one thing. Don't try to clean the entire house. Focus your attention on one room or even one aspect of one room. For example, you could remove any plates from a previous meal that might be on the table. You could sweep up any papers or letters that are left lying around into a single pile. You could arrange the cushions in the seating area and replace the candles from the previous night. Try and put everything back in its correct place. All this is manageable in a five-minute window.

You can repeat this process for each room. The act of tidying not only creates an external environment of calm and hygge, but internally you can feel the stresses that mess and chaos bring with them melting away. You know where everything is and are comfortable that everything has its correct place.

The same habit can be highly effective at the workplace as well. If you are working at a messy desk, where you feel you are drowning under paper or surrounded by used coffee mugs, you are not going to feel particularly productive. Spend five minutes each day organizing your books, papers and workspace so you can prioritize your work accordingly. This will be time well spent and allow you to focus your attention on the most important things in your day with a clear head.

Hygge and You (Habits #10 to #19)

This chapter contains hygge habits which are all about you as an individual. They are designed to be built into your day, at a time which best fits for you. They are activities which you can carry out entirely on your own, allowing you to build a heightened sense of hygge, peace, calm and relaxation within your own living space.

Habit #10 - Be in your favorite space

The chances are you already have a favorite place in your home – somewhere towards which you naturally gravitate when you have a few spare minutes. Somewhere you instinctively feel relaxed and calm and at peace. It might be the kitchen, the living room or perhaps in the garden on a chair in a location which captures the sun most of the day.

My favorite places tend to vary through the seasons. I opt for the garden in the summer, but throughout winter I tend to choose the kitchen and its comforting warmth. I have a chair next to a window where I can read and have a cup of tea in the morning. It probably helps that the dog's bed is there too as she is happy to keep me company whilst I enjoy the calm.

If you're not quite sure where your place would be, take a couple of minutes to ponder where you are drawn to. Think about where you like to sit or where you go just to escape for a little while. Identifying the locations in your home which are perfectly suited to relaxation and feeling warm and comforted is important. It will give you a place to which you can retreat when in need of a little soothing peace and quiet. Get into the habit of using that dedicated place more, even if just for a few extra minutes a day. You could open your daily mail for example, or have your first hot drink of the day in that particular spot.

If you can't think of anywhere at all that currently fits the description, then take a few minutes to look around and consider making a dedicated spot. Add in a textured cushion or two or perhaps a warm blanket. Perhaps it is somewhere in the room with the best view out of the window. Place a book nearby so when you feel like reading, you are doing so in the most comfortable location in your home. Try to make a little place, just for you, that you know will enable you to relax and recuperate in the best possible way.

Habit #11 - Turn off electronic alerts

If you've enabled various electronic alerts on your cell phone or mobile device, then consider turning them off entirely. These alerts, which come from every variety of app on your device, clamor for your attention, demanding that you give precious time up to read them. Alerts from Facebook or twitter or any other social network or email do not need to be opened instantly. If you are having dinner with friends or relaxing with the family, one of the main things that will interfere with a true hygge atmosphere is the incessant and unwelcome beeping of various devices going off.

If you want to check your email, then put aside a certain part of the day to do so. Don't waste time, checking every single email as it comes in. Each time you take out the cell phone, unlock it and mentally process the message, your energies are being diverted needlessly. If you go through your mail in a batch, answering as quickly as you can or deleting emails that need no

15

action, you will save time and be in control of the entire process. Electronic alerts will not interrupt your relaxation or important time spent with real people.

Take just a few minutes to change the settings on your device so you remain undisturbed at home. If you feel you absolutely must check emails outside office hours, then give yourself no more than five minutes to do so.

Habit #12 – Having a hot drink

There are not very many concepts more associated with hygge than a steaming hot cup of tea or coffee which you sip, sitting next to a lovely fire or snuggled up in bed in the warmth. Even the act of putting on the kettle and the promise of warmth and comfort that it brings, is soothing and calming itself.

A hot drink provides an escape from the pressures or stresses of whatever is going on in your life. If you are already used to having a cup of tea or coffee with friends, you will associate the ritual of making tea with happy times, full of laughter and companionship. Even if you are having a five-minute break by yourself, those feelings are still associated with tea and coffee.

Of course, the tea or coffee itself has physical properties which also help to create a feeling of hygge. Try out different varieties such as mint, chamomile, ginseng, lavender or lemon. These are renowned for their highly aromatic flavors as well as medicinal qualities which help to calm and alleviate feelings of stress.

A hot drink therefore has a doubly beneficial effect - a physical and psychological one. That five-minute break to have your warming cup of tea can be highly effective at increasing hygge in your life, at work and at home, alone or with others.

Habit #13 - Reading

Reading is one of my passions. I've read voraciously since I was a child and for me hygge is inextricably linked to the idea of a great book, perhaps with a hot drink by my side. Even in just five minutes, it is possible to immerse yourself in a book and gain a break from the outside world. Reading is a tremendous stress-reliever. A study from the University of Sussex, UK, found that reading for six minutes reduced stress by up to 68% (listening to music and having a cup of tea were also very high on the stress-relieving list).

Reading allows you to become engrossed in another topic of interest or a story, taking you to a place where you can escape worries and anxieties. It has numerous other benefits including increasing vocabulary, being exposed to new ideas and thoughts as well as helping with memory and a general sharpness of the mind.

If you want a little slice of hygge for just five minutes, no matter where you are, sitting down with a great book is one of the most effective ways to achieve it.

Habit #14 - Listen to music

Music has the power to change your mood instantly. It can hold memories of previous events and take you back to happy times. It can evoke all kinds of emotions and has even been found to be able to reduce pain and anxiety after surgery, according to reports from Brunel University, UK, a finding backed up by a similar Danish study. Music has been found to relieve stress in lowering your cortisol levels a hormone which is released into the body when situations have become stressful. When we listen to music we enjoy, it brings with it an emotional response. If we listen to music that feels good to us, we give ourselves a chance to escape from the stresses of the day no matter where we are.

These days it is easy to have music of virtually any description at your fingertips. It might be through music you have stored on a portable device such as a cell phone, it might be through a computer or it could be through one of the many music streaming services that are available.

Of course, your choice of music is a highly individual one. I have a playlist of 20 tracks that I carry with me on various devices. When I am home, I have these songs on vinyl and listen to them in my living room, but I also have them on other formats as well. I have listened to them before important meetings, before I embark on a long task and when I am travelling home at night. There are few opportunities where I can't find a little slice of time for my hygge music.

If you would like some music suggestions, here are some of my favorite hygge tracks. They all hold highly personal memories for me at various stages of my life. I hope you enjoy them, but don't forget to think of your own as well and make it a hygge habit to play one for five minutes when you need it.

- This Must Be the Place – Talking Heads
- Canon in D - Pachelbel (this is a little over 6 minutes but beautiful)
- Air on a G String – J Bach
- Let It Be – The Beatles
- Hallelujah – Jeff Buckley
- Take It Easy – The Eagles
- Three Little Birds – Bob Marley
- Califorina Dreamin' – Mamas and Papas
- The Sound of Silence – Simon and Garfunkel

- Perfect Day – Lou Reed
- Teardrop – Massive Attack
- I Heard it through the Grapevine – Marvin Gaye
- Fast Car – Tracy Chapman
- Imagine – John Lennon

Habit #15 - Cuddle Pets

If you have a pet, you will already be spending a lot more than five minutes looking after him or her which is a great way to bring hygge into the entire family. Cuddling a pet can release similar emotions to those we get with physical contact with people. It can reduce stress hormones such as cortisol and increase levels of serotonin and oxytocin which alleviate. It can also lower cholesterol as well as help your heart.

Stroking your four-legged friend can be so effective that dogs are also used as therapy dogs in nursing homes, for those in physical therapy and for a wide variety of mental health issues including depression and post-traumatic stress disorder.

A further hygge benefit of owning a pet is that they can form a tremendous social bond between family members and friends. They become a talking point for you and for strangers who may feel much more comfortable about striking up a conversation based around your dog than for any other reason. I am frequently stopped by total strangers in the street to ask what breed of dog I have and give her a little stroke. Pets are perfect for breaking down boundaries and will encourage communication and contact between people.

They are an ideal icebreaker and walking them in the same park at the same time each day, even if just briefly, will allow you to meet other like-minded dog owners and form social networks within your own local community. A recent study from the universities of Miami and St. Louis also found that among the many benefits of owning a dog, was becoming more extroverted and comfortable about getting closer to other people.

Any pet requires a considerable amount of attention and looking after. This requires us to think more of other living things than ourselves as well as learning to possess a vast amount of patience and understanding at times! All these positive benefits of pet ownership resonate with the principles of hygge and your pet-stroking habit can bring significant benefits, even in very short periods of time.

Habit #16 - Aromatherapy

Smells can be a huge part of creating hygge. You can use candles or light a couple of reed diffusers in the house to create a pleasingly scented atmosphere. Oils to consider would include frankincense, marjoram, geranium, lemongrass, bergamot, jasmine, ylang ylang or lavender. Be careful to stick to essential oils rather than perfume oils or more generally fragrance oils which can contain various synthetic chemicals.

If you have a little more time at your disposal, then a few drops placed into a hot bath is a great way to relax. You can gain many of the benefits from aromatherapy just by quickly setting up a reed diffuser with your favorite oils. This is a simple daily habit to get into and can be combined with the lighting of candles and setting the right lighting tone in your house at the end of a busy day.

Habit 17 – #Having a footbath

Immersing yourself in a luxurious, bubble-filled, glorious bath with candles casting their flickering illumination sums hygge up perfectly for many people. While it's not impossible to have a five-minute bath, it generally seems a bit of a waste to set it all up, only to spend five minutes in it before you regretfully pull yourself out.

One quick alternative is the footbath. This is a great way to relax after a long day and will help to soothe your aching muscles and reduce inflammation. Using a few drops of essential oil, perhaps lavender for relaxation, will also add to the general ambience. Epsom Salts are another alternative you could consider adding. Even a five-minute soak can really relax your feet and leave you feeling refreshed and calm. It's not quite the same as the full bath experience, but it's a very worthy alternative that takes a fraction of the time.

Habit 18 - #Visualisation

One of the most effective ways to bring more hygge into your life is to imagine yourself doing it – to visualize it occurring. This is a practice that's been adopted by professional athletes for decades who imagine themselves performing a successful action before they actually do it. The effects of this technique are that your brain can understand what you need to do to achieve your goals, before you carry them out in reality. Having completed that action in your mind, you think more positively about your chances of success and therefore are more likely to achieve that goal.

We can use very short periods of visualisation in periods of high stress to relieve tension and transport ourselves to a happier and calmer mental location. The mental side affects our physical reactions. By imagining ourselves to be calmer we gain the appropriate physical reaction as well. We allow that feeling of creating calmness to become more common and natural to us. The process becomes easier and easier the more we do it.

To carry out a five-minute visualization, just make yourself comfortable in a quiet place and close your eyes. Imagine that you are in a place that you find soothing – this could be at home, curled up in front of the fire under a blanket with a great book. It could be on the beach or perhaps walking in a beautiful wood somewhere.

Try and engage with the specifics and imagine particular details. Use all the senses you can – what can you see? Hear? Touch? Smell? Feel? Add as much mental detail as you can and see yourself in that location for a few minutes, enjoying all it has to offer.

This is an easy and effective way to bring peace and calm into your hectic day. Try it just for a couple of minutes a day, whenever it seems appropriate, and you will soon feel the benefits.

Habit #19 - Gratitude journal

A gratitude journal is a wonderful way to record all the things that are good in your life right now. The entries don't have to be long – even a word or two is fine if you like. All you need to do is keep a record of those things in life for which you are grateful. It might be the people in your life to whom you are close. It might be something great that is happening at work or a highly enjoyable social occasion you went to. It might be a song you currently love or a recipe which worked well. It might be a movie or a program on television.

Take a few moments to think about those things that bring you joy, fun, happiness or contentment and note then down. Add a sentence that explains why they have had such a powerful effect on you. It's not something you have to do every day – it is highly effective to re-read previous entries as well and remember those things you enjoyed greatly or treasure.

I like to write when I am warm and cozy in bed, but there is no particular right or wrong time to do it. Add to the journal when the time is right for you. Feeling gratitude is intertwined with wellbeing and hygge. By recording all the good things in your life, you assess the day in positive terms only. You remind yourself of all the good things that have happened that day and the days before it.

Recording your thoughts in a journal allows you to frame the day and finish it on a positive note, leaving you more prepared to face the next day. By writing and reading a journal, just for a short period a day, you give yourself a chance to experience the positive things in your life repeatedly and nothing can be more effective in creating hygge than that.

Hygge and Relieving Stress (Habits #20 to #26)

In order to lead a life with more hygge, it is essential you are able to remove sources of stress from your daily routine. Hygge is often described as making efforts to create a life freed from stresses and anxiety. All the habits below, are designed to do precisely that. Try to build them into your day or week as and when you find appropriate or get into the habit of carrying them out when the situation demands it.

Life is full of various stresses from home to the workplace, from those we put on ourselves to those created by others. Learning how to handle and work through them, having effective mechanisms to cope with stress and allowing yourself to relax and be at your best at all times, is essential for a more hyggeligt life.

Habit #20 - Breathing Exercises

Here is a very easy breathing exercise that will take you no more than five minutes. This quick mindful breathing exercise is designed to allow you simply to focus on the present and be aware of yourself, rather than worry about pressing concerns or stresses in the future. This is a great habit to build into your daily routine and is a wonderful tonic to allow stress to seep away, leaving you more focused and clear-headed. Try it yourself to see how easy and effective it is. These are the simple steps for your five-minute breathing exercise.

1.) Find somewhere comfy to sit where you won't be distracted.

2.) Put a timer on for five minutes and then sit upright. Let your hands rest on your lap and shut your eyes. Let your body relax.

3.) Observe the pattern of your breathing and whatever sensations that brings to your body. Just breathe normally. Note where you can feel your breath. Perhaps in your chest or mouth or nostrils. Just become an observer of your own body breathing.

4.) It's fine if your mind wanders off. Just try and bring it back gently again to your own breath, coming in and then leaving the body.

5.) Carry on until your five minutes is up at which point you can either carry on or slowly open your eyes.

This is a powerfully relaxing exercise. The more we can do to rid ourselves of stress, the more likely we are to bring hygge into our lives.

Habit #21 - Write down your stresses

Taking five minutes to write down concerns is a highly effective way of eliminating stress from your day. You don't have to worry about spelling or grammar – just write down whatever comes into your mind and get it on paper. When writing a journal or diary like this, it is best to use physical pen and paper and to force yourself away from a computer screen.

The very act of removing yourself from electronic devices and sitting alone in a quiet room will allow you to rest. A "stress journal" will allow you to sort out what might be a jumble of confusion in your own mind. When you see things written down on paper, it gives you the chance to sort things through and add previously missing clarity to a situation. You might see answers, whereas all you could see before were problems.

A journal will enable you to see patterns where perhaps previously you viewed the issues of each day as a series of unconnected events. Viewing a sequence of such events over time will help you understand what you need to do or to avoid to prevent certain events occurring at all. A journal becomes a repository for negative thoughts, somewhere for you to write them down and get them out of your system. It is a powerful way to dispel these negative emotions which will only prevent positive thoughts occurring.

Taking five minutes a day, or more if required, for a stress journal is a great habit and time well spent. Getting rid of these negative emotions will allow you then to focus on the positive aspects of your life.

Habit #22 - The Five Minute Exercise Routine

The idea of a steaming cup of coffee and a huge slice of chocolate cake can be very appealing, however a further essential component of hygge is exercise. In Denmark, this can take the form of long walks or various winter sports such as skiing or sledding. The cold weather does not prevent the Scandinavians exercising in almost any weather, which has tremendous health benefits.

These include burning calories, increasing your cardio-vascular strength and all of the accompanying feel-good endorphins that exercise brings with it. The hot drinks and cake can come afterwards as the treat, but physical exercise is essential for a true hygge lifestyle.

Although there is not going to be the time to go for a winter hike in five minutes there are still plenty of activities that you can complete that have a similar effect. Building these into your daily routine will have a highly positive effect on your health and life in general.

There is a huge variety of exercises you can get done in 5 minutes or less. Here is one that I use, mostly in the mornings

1.) Wall Squat – you just need a wall! Place your back to the wall with your hips and knees bent at 90 degrees, as if sitting in chair. Hold that for a minute or if you want extra work, start with your knees and hips just a little bent. After 20 seconds, lower them a little more, then again after another 20 seconds. For the final 20 seconds, position them at the 90-degree angle.

2.) The Plank – get yourself into the push-up position and then bend your elbows so your weight is now on your forearms rather than your hands. You're trying to get your body into a straight line. Try and hold this position for a minute. Take a break half-way through if you need to and then complete the exercise.

3.) Chair Dips – position a chair against the wall so it can't move. Sit down on the front of the chair with your hands behind your hips on the chair's edge, about the width of your shoulders apart. Now raise yourself off the chair and move forward with your feet keeping your chest and head up. Gradually lower yourself down with your arms. The furthest you need to go is until your arms get to a 90-degree bend. Now straighten your arms so they are bearing your body weight. Repeat as many times as you can for a minute.

4.) Step Running – find a step or a slightly elevated platform. Step onto it, right foot then left foot, and then step back off with your right foot followed by your left. Do as many steps as you can for a minute. You can start this exercise by doing 30 seconds, then having a little rest, then the final 30 seconds.

5.) Run on the spot – simply stand where you are with your feet wide apart and knees bent. Then run on the spot as fast as you can for a minute. Pump your arms as well for an additional workout.

These are five exercises which when done regularly will have great benefits both physically and emotionally. They are a great habit to get into at whatever time of day you can manage and will allow you to exercise even if you don't have the time to go for longer walks or extended gym sessions.

Habit #23 - Getting to sleep

If there is one thing that is going to interfere with leading a more hygge life, it is not getting enough sleep. A lack of sleep is linked to many health conditions including heart-related issues, stroke and diabetes. It has been shown to have a detrimental impact on your logic and problem solving skills as well as your cognitive abilities by preventing full concentration and focus.

People who suffer from insomnia are more likely to develop depression and anxiety as well as being more susceptible to tempestuous mood swings, reacting adversely to relatively minor stressful situations. A lack of sleep reduces our ability to cope on a day to day basis which has a knock-on effect on how we feel about ourselves and our own judgement. In turn, feeling anxious and stressed makes it even more difficult to get to sleep in the first place, resulting in even less sleep and this negative cycle continues.

All these emotions and thoughts will prevent any chance of hygge maintaining a hold in your life so it is important to do your best to get an adequate amount of sleep each night (7 -9 hours each night) and to follow some simple habits to give yourself the best chance of deep and effective rest.

Establish a sleep routine that you can stick to – try and get to bed and wake up at the same time each day. This should include work days and days off. This will establish your internal clock so your body will know when it is time to sleep and send the appropriate signals to the body, preparing you for a good night's sleep.

Get into your pre-bed routine – this is a short activity that is designed to relax you and prepare for sleep. It might be a bath or a short read of a book or perhaps writing your journals.

Check the sleeping environment is right – check the bedroom is suitably dark. You could consider using darker curtains to ensure light can't make its way in. Try to eliminate excess noise. You could consider earplugs if you have a partner who snores. Ensure the temperature is right – it is difficult to get to sleep quickly if you are too hot or cold. Ensure the windows have been open at some point during the day to get adequate ventilation and fresh air.

Eating and drinking – it is best to give yourself a chance to digest the evening meal before you get to bed. Don't have a great deal to eat or drink just before it's bedtime and avoid food that might give you indigestion. Substitute your caffeine at night for non-caffeine drinks such as herbal teas.

Following these steps is a relatively simple way to ensure you are giving yourself the best possible chance to maximize your night's sleep. There is no point heading to bed early if you are worried or anxious that you are not going to drop off quickly.

Getting into the right frame of mind for sleep by establishing these quick and painless habits as part of your daily routine will help greatly in gaining more sleep, feeling better both mentally and physically and allowing yourself every chance of gaining more hygge in your life.

Habit #24 - Napping

One of the most common complaints about modern life is the lack of time available for people to complete tasks or do everything they feel they need to do. For many people, the sacrifice they make is to take fewer hours of sleep. Sleeping, however, is essential for many medical and psychological benefits and you do yourself no favors at all when cutting sleep from your daily routine.

In fact, the best action you can take is to actively build sleep into a habit by taking a nap during the day. Taking a nap, ideally late in the morning or early in the afternoon, will help you enormously in getting through the day at your best and leaving you refreshed for the evening. Studies have shown that taking a nap effectively resets your system and will result in a subsequent burst of energy and increased performance.

Sleep consists of five stages that keep repeating during the night, a power nap will include only the first two. Stage one is when your breathing becomes more regular and your heart rate begins to slow.

Stage two involves a light sleep where the muscle activity continues to decrease and your consciousness of the outside world begins to disappear entirely. If you carry sleeping from that point, you enter slow wave sleep for the next two stages and finally Rapid Eye Movement for the final stage which is where most of your dreaming takes place.

By entering stage two sleep during a power nap, even for a short time, you allow yourself to catch up on any sleep you may have missed the previous night as well as giving a boost to your problem solving and learning skills. Reaction times are improved and it can also help with blood pressure and relieving stress. Napping will also improve your mood and allow you to work more productively afterwards, making you more alert and better able to handle the stresses and demands of the rest of the day.

Sleep is critical to our well-being and it is something many of us feel we miss out on. This can lead to tiredness, irritability, under-performance and stress, all of which we are seeking to avoid in our quest for a more hygge lifestyle. Learning to grab a few minutes extra sleep each day as a habit will help you greatly in making you calmer, healthier, more ready to tackle problems and challenges head-on, and ultimately happier.

Habit #25 - Shut your eyes

There are a lot of health benefits to being able just to shut your eyes for five minutes. If you can't grab a quick nap, then sitting quietly with your eyes closed is another viable alternative and a great habit to get into. By closing your eyes, you prevent yourself from looking at things and then processing that visual data into information. You allow yourself to be free from concentrating on anything in particular and you let yourself relax. This has multiple benefits including improving your mood and reducing stress, both of which are important elements of hygge.

Habit #26 - Walk

I have already talked about the importance of exercise and maintaining a healthy lifestyle. Another easy way to build this into a habit is to take a five-minute walk. You may be thinking that you're not going to get very far in five minutes, however it is surprising how much walking frequently for a brief amount of time will add up over the course of a day.

A five-minute walk can have significant health benefits with some reports showing that a quick walk can counteract an hour's worth of sitting down. Researchers at the Mayo Clinic (Rochester, Minn.) showed that walking very short distances often, could be more effective at maintaining health than hitting the gym for an hour.

If you are in the workplace, rather than send an email to a colleague, why not walk over to their desk and have a conversation? Not only do you have that little slice of exercise, but it is likely you will save time by communicating more effectively in person and will be more productive than simply sitting at your desk.

Face to face communication, which can incorporate body language, through which a lot of the meaning of a conversation is conveyed, can be highly effective at building trust and forging cohesive social links between colleagues. This tactic may not be suitable for every occasion (you might need to email twenty people at once or they might be on another continent), but try and introduce it into your working life slowly. Start with just the one walk and conversation rather than an email, and see how it goes.

If you're at home, you could take a quick stroll around your garden to get outside or perhaps pace down your street and back. If you get the bus, try getting off a stop earlier and walking the final five minutes. Walk to a friend's house or the local shop rather than driving. Think of the number of times you might drive a very short distance and see if that can't be replaced just by taking a short walk instead.

This doesn't need to be a massive change in your life, but the accumulation of walking very short distances rather than sitting down, will have numerous health benefits to your heart as well as allowing endorphins to be released into the body. The exercise will also lower cortisol levels which in turn will reduce stress. It will also increase your social connections with people. It's an easy and fun way habit to get into that will add more hygge into your routine.

Hygge and Family (Habits #27 to #33)

It may seem like you spend plenty of time with your family, however much of that may be consumed by various conversations and actions that are critical to keeping a functioning household running, but may not increase any feeling of hygge. There are seemingly hundreds of chores to be carried out within any family and at times it might seem like the household is more of a highly efficient workplace than a comforting home. Each person has their responsibilities and chores which they carry out efficiently, but not necessarily thinking how these activities might be done a little differently or involving others at the same time.

This chapter contains habits that are very quick and take little adjustment to what you might currently do, but are designed to increase the quality of the time that family members spend together. Everyone is still very busy within their own lives, but it can be a relatively easy process to build in some time within schedules for hygge activities and occasions to which every member of the family can look forward and enjoy together.

Habit #27 - Agree on TV

Family time together, without any kind of screen, is wonderful but there is no need to be over-zealous with the banning of films or television entirely. Everyone enjoys watching a great movie or a favorite television show and it can spark off some interesting conversations and topics of discussion.

The trick to make it more of a proper hygge experience is to try and make sure that when the television is on, that everyone is there and enjoying what is on. The worst scenario is that everyone disappears into separate rooms to watch their own show at different times, providing no single point of reference for future conversations or a shared memory.

To work this out, you can spend five minutes as a family agreeing on what can be watched together. The program listings can generally be found online or in a newspaper or if you have access to services like Netflix you can have a quick scroll through the suggested items and see what it comes up with. There may have to be a few compromises here and there, but considering the wealth of television that is on offer these days, it shouldn't be too hard to come up with one or two shows that all the family will watch.

Many programs operate on multiple levels appealing to both children and adults alike, so everyone will be able to enjoy them. Recent examples for our family have been any movie from Disney / Pixar which can operate on multiple levels, appealing to both children and adults alike for different reasons.

Taking the time out together to agree on what will be watched and noting down the times so everyone is aware of the programs is a great way to compromise a little on the screen time and will also add in a sense of anticipation for the date. Add in some candles and hot chocolate for that extra hit of hygge!

Habit #28 - Playing Games

You can always play a game with children for a quick break. Gather them around the table, provide them with a slice of cake and play a quick game such as Snap, Hangman, I Spy, memory games, Charades or 20 Questions. You will quickly find they become used to the routine of being together at a set time, and it enables you to connect and talk to each other at various points during the day.

Children are great at inventing their own games as well. Ask them to come up with a game of their own and explain the rules. This is a great way to get them involved and engage their imagination.

Habit #29 -Coloring In

Another fun activity you can do with children is to grab a coloring book for you to do while the children complete an easier one. Adult coloring books have proved very popular over the past couple of years and can help to lower stress and relax you. While concentrating on coloring, you remove the focus from everyday stresses and concerns. This is not dissimilar to what happens when you meditate or simply sit peacefully in a quiet room.

When you color in with your children, it's another activity that is away from screens and involves you discussing colors, using logic to work out the best choice, seeing patterns and generally being creative together. It's a great way to connect and can be a wonderful, hygge habit.

Habit #30 - Laugh

Laughter is one of the quickest and easiest ways to make your life less stressful and more hyggeligt. It gets your heart pumping, reduces tension and releases endorphins into the body.

You can find laughter in a number of places. The first of these is everyday life. Be on the watch for things that are amusing – it is surprising how much you will see when you deliberately start to look out for it. Trying not to take life overly seriously and being able to laugh at yourself will enable you to find humor wherever you are.

Secondly, you can find humor by searching for it. Potential locations include websites, books, magazines, cartoons, short videos or emails. Discovering a comedian or a book that you find funny will give you a chance for a quick burst of laughter wherever you are. One of my favorite books of all time is Catch 22 by Joseph Heller which is a true comic work of genius. I have multiple copies of it at home and work and have given a copy to all my friends and family. Even when I think of it now, it brings a smile to my face and makes me feel good. If you can find something similar, then you will be able to bring humor and laughter into your life easily and make the day a little more hyggeligt.

We also tend to find more humor and laughter when together with people in social situations. Telling stories to friends, even (or perhaps especially) at your own expense, can be a great way to give everyone a chance to laugh. It will also give you something else to remember next time you are reminiscing about the gathering and laugh at again.

One of the funny things about laughter is that even forced laughter has numerous benefits. Even making yourself laugh, without finding anything amusing in particular, can bring health benefits. Try it yourself now – just smile and then laugh for 10 to 20 seconds.

You may well feel a little stress relief, a little boost to your day. We can trick our body into making us feel more relaxed and better by fake laughter, even if it's not the real thing. You will often find that your fake laughter very quickly gives way to real laughter, which may explain why we get the benefits no matter what kind of laughter we indulge in.

Habit #31 - Turn off screens

It is amazing how much of our lives is dominated by screens of one type or another. From the large television you may have at home to your computer monitor at work to the ever-present cell phone in your pocket, we have become accustomed to having information and entertainment at our fingertips at all times.

Unfortunately, this ease of access to information can often come at the expense of time spent with "real" people in "real life", as well as having its own adverse medical effects. There are numerous studies showing that excessive screen time affects sleep patterns and subsequently focus and attention at school or at work.

Too much screen time can lead to a more sedentary lifestyle which has its own resulting health problems. Vision can be impaired from gazing at a small screen for too long with inadequate breaks. There can be further medical issues with joints in the fingers or repetitive motion syndrome. On a social level, people can become less able to interact in real life, preferring instead the relative anonymity of online communications.

Having a period in your day and the family's day where you can insist on no screen time at all is critical. Start with just five minutes. Insist that everyone, children and adults, have put down their electronic devices and that the television is off. You could also specify that devices are banned from certain rooms entirely.

Once you have established this rule, you will find that people are more willing to engage in conversation and effective communication, especially children who are quite happy to talk about their day and their achievements when given a proper platform to do so. This allows everyone to share in each other's lives, perhaps over a cup of tea and a biscuit, or over dinner together at the table for longer periods.

Giving a focus to this conversation lends it an importance and will prioritize this period for the entire family. Even if it is only for five minutes at a time, it is invaluable for strengthening family bonds and friendships.

Habit #32 - Schedule a family meal

Take five minutes to ensure that you can hold a family meal where everyone can get together. Getting many people around the same table at the same time is often difficult, especially as children grow older and have various school or social commitments of their own. However, it is important to try and establish a time when everyone can meet to have a chat and share a meal, even if it's not going to happen every day.

One effective way of checking times, is to set up a calendar where everyone can add their regular dates and times of various commitments. This can be done online, but is equally effective with a large wall calendar which can be updated. Once you have a night established, then let everyone know so each person is aware of the time and place.

I am a great fan of theme nights as well (e.g. pasta night or taco night or pizza night) which makes the dinner special. Another way of arranging the menu is to make a list of the top 20 family favorite meals. This way you know something can be cooked that will be popular with everyone.

As well as the time spent eating the meal, the time spent preparing it can also be important. Arrange for different people to make their own contributions – possibly an entire course, but even if they are just in the kitchen helping, then that will mean everyone is working well together. Allocate tasks beforehand, so everyone is clear where their responsibilities lie.

If you wanted to make it even more of a social occasion every now and then, you could also invite your neighbors. Perhaps make an ongoing arrangement where you all pitch in and cook something for each other once a month.

By spending less than five minutes arranging a meal together, which everyone will enjoy, you create the opportunity for a lovely dinner, as well as the anticipation of the meal. This is a great way to get everyone together to share a meal and connect over good food and drink.

Habit #33 - Cooking

Food and drink and eating meals together are very important for hygge, however the making of the meal can be just as important as its consumption. When you are cooking with others, you are focused, you are following instructions on a recipe and you can teach children about measurements and weights and ingredients. It's a great learning experience and is also tremendous fun to do together – kids generally adore cooking, especially if you are making something they find delicious.

Recipes don't have to be long and complex to taste good – a five-minute recipe can be made at any time with the minimum of fuss. Look for recipes with few ingredients that require very little cooking. Despite the short timeframe, you can make some wonderful delicacies that the whole family will enjoy as well as being a little quirky and different.

One example I make is the cake in a mug. There are lots of different recipes for various flavors, but if chocolate is the fancy of the day, then try this. Add three tablespoons of flour, two tablespoons of sugar, two tablespoons of cocoa powder and half a teaspoon of baking powder into a microwave-safe mug. Mix together and then add three tablespoons of milk, three tablespoons of vegetable oil and if you want to go the extra mile, some chocolate chips. Stir it all again and then pop it into the microwave for 90 seconds. Voila! The five-minute chocolate cake!

Here's another favorite which can take even less time. Take a banana and slice it lengthways, almost all the way through. Add chocolate chips down the middle and whatever else you fancy. Wrap the banana in aluminum foil and place it in the pre-heated oven for five minutes or until the chocolate has melted. You can also grill it if you prefer. Add a little cream or ice-cream for a lovely treat that takes barely any time to prepare.

You will no doubt be able to create your own, personalized favorites but there are many other different five minute recipes you can make with the minimum of fuss. This is a great hygge activity for the entire family and will quickly turn from a habit into a tradition. We tend to do a lot of our baking on a Saturday afternoon and it becomes a little period of the week to which everyone looks forward.

You can fit the five-minute bake in whenever you have the time and it is a hygge habit that the entire family will truly savor. You can even get your adult guests to give it a go and bake their own desert when they come for dinner!

Hygge and Friendship (Habits #34 to #42)

One of the principal features of hygge is the concept of friendship and social interaction, a feeling of belonging and in a wider sense being part of a community that looks after each other. We all know how easy it can be to let friendships slide due to the stresses of too much work or simply feeling tired at the end of a busy working week. Before too long, it has been a couple of months or more since you met with people, purely for social reasons, and this can lead to an increased feeling of loneliness and isolation.

This idea of social interaction can be with both local friends and neighbors, but it shouldn't exclude friends who have moved away. Maintaining those close ties is important, both for you and your friends, and making a little effort to stay in touch will allow you and them to feel good. It will remind them that they are still important and that you care about them.

The following quick and easy hygge habits will enable you to build and strengthen those ties of friendship that add so much to our lives. Try and build them into your weekly routine, make the activities into a habit and see how they bring about the positive feelings from hygge, both for you and your friends.

Habit #34 - Call A Friend

One easy way to stay in touch is a quick phone call. A lot of people end up putting this off because they feel they don't have the time or the energy to indulge in a long chat. However, this doesn't need to be an hour-long conversation. A quick call can be just as effective to show that you are still thinking of friends of family even in their absence. Set aside a good five minutes of your time to make the call. Don't try and complete other tasks at the same time - make the call worthwhile and valuable by giving up a little of your own time. By making the effort to call, you are reminding them they are still important and that you care.

This is an easy step to take that takes very little time, but can be most effective at re-establishing and reaffirming links with friends or family you don't see all the time. Try and build it into your week so you can chat to one person you haven't spoken to in a while. See how the conversation goes and where it leads to in strengthening links. You can always follow it up with a quick card to say how great it was to hear from them again and arrange a time to meet in person next time they're around.

Habit #35 - Send a postcard

Another easy way to stay in contact with friends who have moved away is simply to send a quick postcard. It doesn't have to be a purchased card. You will often find free cards at various cafes or museums or shops. I always take one from my local cinema which likes to advertise their coming movies with a free postcard. If I see a film that I know a friend would have loved to have seen, I write down a few words and send it off.

The effect of this is that it shows I'm thinking of him or her, that I remember previous shared experiences and enjoyable times and that I've given up a little of my time to make the effort. Getting a letter through the post, addressed to you that isn't a bill or junk mail, is still a little pleasure for most people. If they have kids, you can address it to them as well, as they are normally delighted to receive a letter.

A written letter lacks the immediacy of an email, but has more of an emotional impact. Imagine how pleased you would be to get a letter from a friend of family member who has moved away but still often thinks of you. This is an extremely simple activity that takes even less than five minutes, but can have a powerful effect and will bring hygge into the life of both you as the sender and that of your recipient.

Habit #36 - Arrange a meeting

Take two or three minutes to arrange some kind of meeting with a friends of a group of friends. The easiest way to do this is probably through your cell phone with either a SMS message or if you have apps such as WhatsApp you can arrange to meet as a group. This way everyone in the group can see your messages and reply to everyone at the same time.

Set up a specific time and date to meet and have a coffee or a meal or go see a movie. Set the date a couple of weeks away so everyone has adequate time to make childcare provision or check their diary. This should take no more than five minutes to arrange. You now have the added pleasure of being able to look forward to the meeting and then catching up with friends.

Most of the time, you will find people are eager to meet up, but end up putting it off for one reason or another. If you can take the initiative and spend five minutes arranging the date, you will find everyone grateful for your actions.

Habit #37 - Send a thank-you card

If you've shared dinner at a friend's house, then take five minutes just to send a quick thank you card. These days, the written card seems to slowly disappearing, however whenever I have received one, it's been something I've cherished.

A thank you note doesn't have to be a massive letter. Just jot down your thoughts expressing your gratitude for the evening's hospitality and send it off. You don't need to use any kind of formal language. Anything that is a genuine expression of thanks is perfect.

Thank you letters can be very simple. Start with "thank you for dinner / your kind gift / whatever it is". Then add a sentence explaining why you enjoyed the meal or the gift ("it was wonderful to catch up and hear your news"). Finally, add a sentence about meeting up again in the not too distant future. For example, you could invite your friends to dinner at your own house the following month. You could put an invitation down to have a coffee out at that café you talked about over dinner.

Hygge is all about cementing relationships and solidifying social cohesion. A quick thank you card allows you to keep communication open, as well as showing that you care enough to go to the bother of writing things down on paper and sending a letter. It's a quick and easy way to keep friendships alive and strong.

Habit #38 - Eat cake

Perhaps Hygge is not about being abstemious or denying yourself things that are going to make you happy, so it is important that you can apply this equally to food as to other

46

areas of life. If you are out with a friend, a slice of chocolate cake as a treat for example, could be the perfect hygge pick-me-up. A five-minute slice of deliciousness, a little taste of chocolatey heaven, can go a long way.

Enjoying food, truly savoring it, is important. You don't need to go crazy, but having a slice of cake as a conscious treat for yourself is absolutely fine. Indeed, recent research has concluded that continually depriving yourself of what you desperately crave will not help you lose weight. In the end, your willpower will dip and you will end up binge eating on the "forbidden" food. Having a little treat when you want one will aid in sticking to a reasonable eating plan.

Habit #39 - Do a quiz

Another five-minute activity which can promote hygge in a number of ways is to have a brief period in the day when you can complete a small puzzle. This could be anything from a quick crossword to a word or number game, or perhaps a general knowledge quiz of ten questions.

I once worked at a packaging design company for two years when I first started my career. Every working day at 10:45 in the morning, there would be a meeting spot where four or five of us would convene and complete a short quiz in the newspaper over a cup of coffee.

It gave us a chance to meet, get to know each other, make friends and it became an opportunity to take our minds off the current work. In addition to that, we also learned a lot about each other – as well as a wealth of general knowledge. Even now, I remain in contact with many of the friends I made there and although we live a long way apart, we continue to make the effort to stay in touch.

A simple, but regular meeting to complete a puzzle or a quiz, unrelated to work, will give you a chance to exercise your brain in a different way as well as to share a laugh and a break with friends. Even if you just do it by yourself, it will remain something to look forward to, something fun to anticipate each day and provide a welcome break from the task you may have been carrying out.

Habit #40 - Singing

I'm the first to admit my voice is not great by any means, however I love singing along to a tune that is playing on the radio or from my own music collection. The great news is that singing is not only fun, but releases endorphins which reduce your stress level and can increase self-esteem. In addition, the act of singing releases oxytocin which is a stress-reliever. Singing is a great exercise which has the added benefit of increasing oxygen levels as well as improving your posture as you need to stand up straight to get air into the diaphragm.

The opportunities for singing probably come along more than you think. You could sing along in the car or even in the shower or at home as you are listening to music. If you are with friends in a group out or at home, a sing-along with karaoke can be great fun.

If you want to take it a step further, you can also sing in groups such as organized choirs which will give you another chance to meet people, increase your confidence and make friends. Singing together is, unsurprisingly, a very popular activity in Denmark. Rest assured that you don't have to be a wonderful singer to reap all the benefits that singing brings. Give it a go and you will be surprised how good you feel with each tune you blast out.

Habit #41 - Dancing

Perhaps if you're at work then flinging yourself around the office might not be the most immediate route to promotion, but if you're alone or with those you feel comfortable, then indulging in a short five-minute dance might be the best thing you do all day. It's no surprise that both singing and dancing are core fundamentals of Danish culture and social gatherings.

Dancing to your favorite tune is a tremendous form of exercise, that will get both your heart pumping and improve your aerobic fitness as well. It will also resonate on a more emotional level, with various studies showing that dancing, in all its various forms, can reduce anxiety and stress and boost self-esteem. We dance because it feels good. You can try it with some headphones on or just turn up your favorite song and dance away.

If you have a longer, then dancing is a great way to forge social connections as well – either with a partner or more generally with a wider group of people. Dancing with other people, all to the same beat, is a great way for everybody to connect and interact.

Build five minutes into your day to take a quick dance, alone or with another person, and you will find it a most enjoyable way to build up fitness and release all forms of stress.

If you are singing and dancing either by yourself or together with friends, then the final step is to play the instrument yourself! Listening to and making music is a great work out for your brain. You need to read the notes, translate the music on the page into a physical action and then try and lend an emotional interpretation of your own to the music.

It requires focus and concentration and will enable you to put aside the stresses and concerns of the day just for a short period. As well as being relaxing it helps with memory, logic and your speed of thinking. It is also ideally suited to frequent, short periods of activity so by indulging in five minutes a day solid practice you can see some impressive improvement quite rapidly.

This can be a lovely thing to do together as a group, especially after a dinner, with a warm drink and with everyone in generally good spirits. Having everyone sing along to a tune, while you are accompanying on the piano or the violin or the saxophone, is a great way to entertain and make all your audience become active participants. The whole process strengthens ties and aids with communication. It is also, quite simply, great fun.

How to ensure Hygge becomes a way of life

All the practices described above are designed to bring more hygge into your life – for you and for all those around you. They remove stress and promote a calm and loving atmosphere at home or at work.

These are actions that will work best when repeated over time. They will achieve more as they are built into your schedule and when used together, will have a powerful, cumulative effect on your life. They can all be practised within a small timeframe of five minutes or less. They don't need a special time or place, nor do they need to be completed every day. You can of course just pick and choose the ones you think will be most useful to you on any particular day or week.

Time

What if I don't have 5 minutes?

All the habits in the book can be completed within five minutes, however there will also be significant benefits to carrying them out even on a much smaller timeframe. Walking just for a minute will help, as will reading or listening or dancing or arranging a get-together or lighting just one candle or watering just one plant or arranging just one corner of one room just the way you like it.

If you only have just a very short amount of time, you can still start many of the activities in this book. You will find yourself less stressed, more relaxed and better able to bring every element of hygge into your life in all its various forms.

Can I practise these habits for longer?

These activities can be extended as long as you wish. You don't need to limit yourself necessarily to five minutes for each. If you have more time, if you are enjoying practising these activities, if you and your family feel you are enjoying the benefits of a more hygge life, then carry on as long as you like. Go for longer walks, communicate with more people for longer, arrange more social gatherings, arrange more rooms that can fully embrace hygge principles and allow yourself to gain the rewards of doing so.

The beauty of all the activities I have talked about is that you will get highly significant benefits for yourself, yet each one can be completed in a short time. However, they are flexible as well and you will find yourself enjoying a much more hyggeligt and joyful lifestyle by practising them for short or for long periods.

How can I make these habits stick?

Everything that has been talked about in this book is a hygge habit that has been designed to fit into your routine and make your life easier and more enjoyable. These habits will generally stick with you naturally because the benefits will be immediately obvious and you will enjoy doing them.

However, there are occasions of course, when it can feel difficult to implement habits because of time constraints or pressure from work or other unforeseen factors. There will be always be the odd circumstance that might pop up that prevents you carrying out the activities that you want. Here are some further tips that will enable you to make your hygge habits stick.

Be clear with yourself and your family

One of the habits mentioned in the book is being able to abandon screen time in favor of face-to-face communication. It's possible that you might receive some resistance from others when carrying this out.

If that turns out to be the case, then have a discussion between you all about why you think it's a good idea and what the prospective benefits will be. Don't try to issue edicts from above, but do your best to get everyone on board and moving in the same direction as you.

You will find it much easier if everyone understands why they are doing it, rather than resenting what's going on without any understanding. Get people on your side and working with you by communicating what you are trying to achieve and why it's important for everyone.

Habit timings

When you try implementing a better sleep pattern or reading more often or any of the activities above, then give it some time to see the positive results come in and what the effects are of living a more hygge life. Equally, if you try and don't manage it a few times, then persevere. Keep trying and progress will become much easier.

Many of these hygge habits will work best if implemented daily. For example, it will be far more effective to get a good night's sleep every night than every second or third night. The effects of using stress or gratitude journals become positively compounded the more you use them. Breathing exercises become easier and more effective the more you try them.

Of course, not every habit is applicable daily, such as sending a thank you card for a meal (although making that a habit after every meal is a great one to do), but if possible, think about making time to carry out habits every day.

Use trigger events for your habits

Another useful idea is to use other events as a reminder to yourself to carry out that particular habit. I mentioned above that whenever I go to cinema, I grab a free postcard to send to a friend to say hello. For me, the very act of going to a movie reminds me to take a card, so it is now second nature for me to have a stamp and a pen just so I can send it off quickly.

If I have an important meeting coming, I know I need just a couple of minutes for breathing and visualization. When my children come home, they know to come into the kitchen where I can give them a snack and we can talk for five minutes about their day.

All these hygge habits can be strengthened by using trigger events which you will be able to find as you go through your own day. It becomes part of your routine to the point where you no longer actively think about the habits. They become inbuilt into your lifestyle and will, with no conscious effort on your behalf, automatically bring the benefits of hygge into your day.

Hygge habits are reinforcing

One of the most effective and powerful things about the habits I have talked about is that they are all able to strengthen each other. For example, getting into the habit of starting a sleep routine earlier will enable you to feel better and calmer the next day. In turn, this will make you more effective and productive. You will achieve more in less time thereby allowing you more time to carry out whichever of the various activities you like, for example reading or listening to music or spending more time with your family.

Breathing exercises can go together with visualization techniques to eliminate stress and anxiety. This is reflected in how you feel internally for yourself and how you appear externally to others. Being freed of stress, feeling calmer, happier, more relaxed, safer, feeling in general more hygge, allows you to create hygge in your own home for others to experience. It also means you will be able to get to sleep faster and sleep for longer and more refreshing periods, gaining the benefits there again.

Each of the habits in this book are designed to strengthen each other and they work best when combined with each rather than in isolation. The cumulative effect of multiple habits carried out daily is substantial and will enable you to live a much greater hygge lifestyle more quickly.

Observe the benefits of hygge habits

It is a highly worthwhile process every now and then just to take a step back and see how effective your new habits have been. Note the changes in your own daily life and those around you. For example, you could consider your extra energy levels from more sleep or stronger social connections being made between friends and family from more frequent conversations and family time.

Simply by observing all the positive effects of the habits in this book, you will feel even more encouraged to continue to make every area of your life more receptive to the benefits of hygge habits.

Conclusion

Hygge is a word that defies a truly accurate translation into English - it is a combination of togetherness, contentment, joy, feeling warm and safe, companionship and feeling at peace with yourself and the world. All the hygge habits that I have talked about in this book are designed to allow you to bring more hygge into your personal and professional lives. Each is simple enough to be completed within a very short period, yet the repercussions are significant.

Each of these habits can be carried out wherever and whenever you wish – the more frequently they are engaged with and practised, the more effective they will be. The more you can build them into your daily life or weekly routine, the more easily a hygge atmosphere and lifestyle can be created for you and your friends and family.

The benefits of hygge are several and significant. The hygge habits in this book will reduce your stress and worries and allow you to focus more on the things that truly matter to you. They will enable you to lead a happier, more content life that holds more time for you, for your family and your friends. Hygge is a concept which stresses the value of the simpler things in life – social gatherings, feeling belonging to those closest to you and to the community in which you live, a sense of comfort and security and safety. All these feelings are enhanced through your hygge habits.

These feelings and aspirations are often ideals that are discarded in today's society, with its never-ending hustle and bustle to obtain more, to spend more, to get the latest version of something you already have. These are targets thrust at us every day, through every advertising medium you can think of. They are presented to us as the only way to create happiness, as if buying the latest cell phone or car will somehow add a feeling of completeness to our lives.

I hope that through this book I have shown that one of the reasons why the Danish are top of the world's leader board when it comes to happiness and contentment as a nation, is that they discard these meaningless messages in favor of the pursuit of the hygge ideals. The fact that hygge is built into the country's DNA, that it is part of who they are, that everyone understands what it is, even if everyone doesn't all come up with the same dictionary definition for the word, means that as a nation, they understand the importance of the simpler things in life.

They make time for gatherings of family and friends. They make the effort to create and nurture a local community that can work together for each other. They know that how important it is to try to minimize or remove every source of stress in life.

All the hygge habits in this book have been described with those same aims in mind. They are designed to achieve the same targets in your life that have been part of the Danish culture and lifestyle for generations. They can all be embedded into your daily routine or weekly activities easily and quickly and, working together, will serve to create more hygge in your life, starting today.

With the habits in this book, you will soon find that hygge becomes part of your own life as a matter of course. You will find that all the actions you take as routine will work together to create a less stressed, happier, and far more content and satisfying life for you every single day. And nothing can possibly be more hygge than that.

More books by the author

I very much hope you have truly enjoyed reading this book. If you would like to read more about hygge and its benefits for you, please take a look at my other hygge books below and more to follow.

48614317R00034

Made in the USA
San Bernardino, CA
30 April 2017